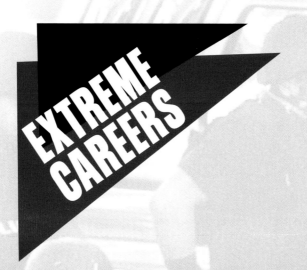

POLICE SWAT TEAMS
Life on High Alert

Christopher D. Goranson

the rosen publishing group's
rosen
central

This book is dedicated to the men and women in law enforcement everywhere who put their lives at risk in the line of duty. Special thanks to Bob Brown, Linda Suttle, and Brandon Petitt for their help in writing this book.

Published in 2003 by The Rosen Publishing Group, Inc.

29 East 21st Street, New York, NY 10010
Copyright © 2003 by The Rosen Publishing Group, Inc.

First Edition

Library of Congress Cataloging-in-Publication Data

Goranson, Christopher D.
Police SWAT teams : life on high alert / Christopher D. Goranson.—1st ed.
p. cm. — (Extreme careers)
Summary: Portrays job-related experiences that are typical of police officers who serve the public as SWAT team members.
Includes bibliographical references and index.
ISBN 0-8239-3635-X (lib. bdg.)
1. Police—Special weapons and tactics units—Juvenile literature. 2. Police—Vocational guidance—Juvenile literature.
[1. Police—Special weapons and tactics units.—Vocational guidance. 2. Vocational guidance.] I. Title. II. Series.
HV8080.S64 G67 2003
363.2'32—dc21

                                                              2001008118

Manufactured in the United States of America

Contents

Come Out with Your Hands in the Air!

*J*ust moments ago dispatch received a call from police officers responding to a silent alarm at a local bank. An armed robbery is in progress, and you and your SWAT (Special Weapons and Tactics) team members are on the way. You've been alerted that both the suspects and some civilian hostages are still inside the building, which is now being surrounded by other police officers as they reach the scene. When you arrive at the command post that has been established in a nearby office building, you hear the sound of a police helicopter in the distance. It was sent to offer visual assistance for your team. Hours pass as a police negotiator tries to convince the suspects to release their hostages, but they are *refusing. It looks as if SWAT will have to go in and attempt to free the hostages. You put on your gear and go through a last check of your equipment. As your team prepares its approach to the building, you make your entrance through the front door in groups of four and then cover the side entrances in pairs. When you enter through one of the side doors, a well-dressed man who has his hands in the air suddenly approaches you. He is unarmed. As you instruct the other units to stand by at their positions, you confirm that the man really is the bank manager, as he says. The manager recounts the facts of the situation and offers you information about the layout of the building and where he last saw the suspects. You relay the information directly to your incident commander back at the command post, and he gives you the green light to proceed. Your team determines approach tactics and agrees on sectors of fire, then enters the main bank lobby. Upon entering, you find two women crouched behind a nearby desk; one of them yells, "What's going on? Help us! What is happening to us?" The two women appear to be customers, but you aren't so sure. You keep your weapon on the two women, confirm your sector with your partner, and demand that the women place their hands on the desk. Then, as your partner closely watches the second woman, who appears fearful, you tell both women to lie on the floor. The one who was asking all of the questions refuses. She immediately demands to leave the bank. You persist with the women until both finally obey and the main lobby is secured. Suddenly, you notice something that was hidden from your view: Both women had weapons within easy reach under the desk, but because you and your partner diligently controlled the situation and demanded that they lay down, you isolated the threat. A bell sounds and your supervisor comes down from an observatory position above. "Good job," he says. "You have passed your training mission. Had you not remembered your skills or communicated poorly with the other officers, this scenario could have ended much differently."*

Special Forces Next Door?

A SWAT team is a select team of law enforcement officers who are highly trained for very
dangerous situations. Sometimes, SWAT teams are
called Special Emergency Response Teams or SERT,
Special Tactics and Rescue or STAR, Emergency
Response Teams or ERT, or simply, tactical teams.
The SWAT team can be considered the "major
league" of a police department, where only the best
and brightest officers are accepted. These men and
women must train for extremely dangerous situations
such as bank robberies, hostage crises, and conflicts
where civilians are in danger of coming into contact
with terrorists. Because of this, SWAT team officers

train for many different scenarios, or situations, so they are prepared to handle any type of crisis.

For example, a SWAT team may continuously practice how best to rescue people from a dangerous situation, or how to calmly convince bank robbers to surrender without harming themselves or others. When all other methods fail, SWAT team officers are prepared to do whatever is necessary to protect civilians' lives.

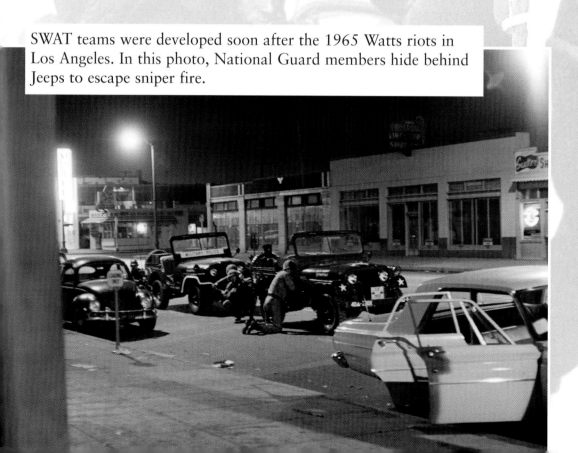

SWAT teams were developed soon after the 1965 Watts riots in Los Angeles. In this photo, National Guard members hide behind Jeeps to escape sniper fire.

A Texas Department of Public Safety patrolman looks through the scope of his rifle at the University of Texas Tower observation deck, where a sniper shot and killed fourteen people on August 1, 1966.

SWAT teams and other special tactics units were first established in the mid–1960s. After the Watts riots—a six-day spree of violence in Los Angeles that left thirty-four people dead and hundreds injured—and the University of Texas sniper attack—when fourteen people were fatally shot by Charles Whitman in Austin in 1966—police departments felt an urgent need to create a specialized force of officers.

The original SWAT teams were developed to deal with these very dangerous or highly volatile situations, or others like them. These events required that the officers involved make no mistakes. To help this effort, police departments began training special crews or groups of officers for specialized missions where the lives of hundreds could be endangered.

Throughout history, different types of law enforcement specialists have always been valuable. For instance, the United States armed forces use groups like the Navy Seals or the Army Rangers for similar tasks of extreme danger. The army even has its own hostage rescue team, the ultrasecret Delta Force. Governments in other countries also have special tactical teams ready to assist them when serious trouble arises. These highly trained teams must be flexible because they cannot always predict what kind of crisis they will have to control.

SWAT teams are made up of talented police officers who are experts at certain skills. For example, some officers are excellent marksmen, meaning that they are very skilled with firearms. These men and women might someday begin training to support SWAT team members as snipers, or expert shooters who target enemies from concealed positions. Others may be savvy communicators who act as expert negotiators between individuals during crisis situations. These people are effective when discussing demands and issues with criminals even if they are psychologically impaired. They may save lives simply by helping a suspect come to terms with what he or she has done and convince him or her to surrender peacefully. Other officers might be especially useful in rescue situations. These men and women perform well in stressful environments. Others may have had previous experience in the military. Any of these skills are useful for men and women who want to become SWAT team officers.

Safety, Diligence, and Control

Occupations in the field of law enforcement require the work of qualified, dedicated people. Police officers must display the authority of their positions when dealing with hostile and aggressive people, and hazardous situations. SWAT members must pass physical tests, as one officer's lapse in alertness during a mission can spell trouble—or even disaster—for the entire team. They must also pass intelligence tests.

Police SWAT Teams: Life on High Alert

SWAT teams largely succeed because of the time they take to plan their approach. Officers must never act emotionally and must always make every effort to save lives. A talented SWAT member should be even-tempered, self-disciplined, and efficient.

Because SWAT teams are designed to help the police department in extremely risky situations, officers must perform well during moments of great stress, such as when someone is being held at gunpoint, or when

A SWAT team moves in on a houseboat on the waterway along Miami Beach during a manhunt for the killer of fashion designer Gianni Versace in 1997.

many lives are at risk in public buildings, such as stadiums or arenas. SWAT officers must go through rigorous training exercises and be willing to tackle difficult challenges. SWAT officers are men and women who do their jobs with professionalism, discretion, and efficiency.

To help officers make split-second decisions, they spend time learning effective problem-solving and safety techniques. This is done in order to improve their quick response reflexes. After all, a rapid response is often one of the most valuable tools when protecting innocent civilians in the midst of a dangerous situation. Minimizing public risk is the key reason SWAT teams exist today.

Street SWAT

SWAT team officers don't only lead the way in a dangerous situation. Some SWAT teams are used for crime suppression, where officers who are not on call-up or in training are used to patrol crime-ridden areas. These teams are usually searching for specific threats that have affected a particular area, such as by a terrorist organization or gangs. In other more typical examples, a crime suppression team may patrol a neighborhood that has seen an increasing amount of carjackings or robberies.

SWAT team officers who are on call-up must make themselves available instantly, twenty-four hours a day, and be prepared to perform well no matter when their services are requested. Because of this, officers must be mentally prepared to protect the public at all times, even if it means sacrificing their personal time.

Practice Makes Perfect

2

Chances are you already have an impression in your mind about a SWAT team member's job. Most people probably picture SWAT officers rushing into dangerous situations to rescue a hostage or catch a suspect.

But what really happens when SWAT teams are needed? Many times officers must wait, sometimes for hours on end, without taking any action at all. Hostage negotiations may last for days at a time in the most extreme circumstances. When the time does come to act, however, a SWAT team officer aims to subdue a suspect without a single shot being fired. Officers attempt a quiet and undetected entry, taking criminals into custody before they even realize they are under surveillance. Other times, SWAT teams might negotiate a lengthy surrender with a suspect, still ensuring that he or she remains uninjured. SWAT teams work very hard to control situations before they disrupt public safety. Real-life events, however, play out very differently than they do in a video game or movie.

Being a member of a SWAT team means much more than just getting the bad guys. In rural areas, officers sometimes perform search and rescue operations more than any other task. And unlike how they are portrayed during a video game, real search and rescue missions allow only one chance to make an appropriate decision. As a result, SWAT officers have to train endlessly to make appropriate, split-second decisions in a crisis. If an officer makes a wrong decision, it could cost lives. Because of this, SWAT officers have to be extremely careful. They must remain aware of their surroundings at all times.

In order to prepare for even the most unusual of situations, SWAT team officers undergo rigorous practice drills. These sessions are meant to make situations as realistic as possible, so officers will be ready when a real crisis arises.

Back to School

Even after high school and college, a potential police officer continues his or her education. A prospective officer must apply to be accepted into a police academy, where he or she is trained in general policing duties such as evaluating a situation, interviewing a suspect, or making an arrest. Once a cadet graduates from the academy, he or she must pass an exam called the

Cadets hit the books at a class at the Pennsylvania State Police Academy in Hershey, Pennsylvania.

Police Officer Standard Test (POST). After passing the POST, he or she may search for a job opening on a police force, competing with other would-be officers for any potential job. Even after obtaining that position, it may still be years before an officer can join a tactical force. Because of the high standards sought from SWAT officers, they must pass additional tests and psychological examinations, and undergo specialized training for that specific force. Members on a SWAT team must rely on one another under every circumstance. This cooperation and interdependence requires great dedication from all SWAT members.

Proving Ground

Training is essential to a SWAT team's effectiveness. It not only helps keep officers sharp, but also improves working relationships. Just like any other team, practice always enhances a team's performance. Some SWAT team drills focus on perfecting certain skills, such as shooting a variety of firearms. SWAT team members are generally required to maintain shooting skill accuracy of more than 90 percent.

An officer with the Tennessee Police Tactical Unit demonstrates an upside-down rappelling technique used to peer into windows from above.

Other drills focus on team building, communication methods, and efficiency techniques to increase speed and safety. To do this, academies often utilize tire house drills, exercises that improve safety while under fire and other challenging situations.

Tire houses, or training areas surrounded on all sides by walls of used tires, are used to train SWAT members in search techniques and other tactics. Many tire house areas have elevated platforms or bridges that allow instructors to view officers' training firsthand.

Real house drills are practice techniques that occur in an actual house on the training grounds. These drills teach officers what to consider when an actual live entry into a residence is required. All of these elements are realistic and stress the importance of concentration.

Often, active or retired military experts are hired to help train potential SWAT members. The training received from these individuals is valuable because of the similarities between the activities of military forces and SWAT teams. Heckler and Koch, the company that manufactures the popular submachine gun favored by the Navy Seals and many SWAT teams, also offers specialized training.

Inside a SWAT Team

3

Each SWAT team member has different responsibilities. A SWAT team's basic five-person unit is called an element. The element consists of a team leader, a scout, a rear guard, and two assaulters. Each member of the team has specific responsibilities and skills, just like members of any other team. There is a team captain (the leader), the offense (the assaulters), and a defense (the guard).

The general five-person unit of the Los Angeles Police Department (LAPD) SWAT consists of a leader, a scout, a guard, and two assaulters. The leader is responsible for making the initial dynamic (sudden) entry. At the same time, the assaulters provide backup and secure the cleared areas. A sniper and spotter may also assist the element as needed, along with additional law enforcement personnel.

Meet the Element

Different police departments use various team configurations or arrangements depending on each unique situation. Generally, the element positions are designated as follows.

SWAT teams from southern New Jersey police departments undergo special training at Trump World's Fair Casino in Atlantic City in 1999.

The Scout

The scout is the advance person for an entry team. His or her job is to gather information before the element enters a building or any other officers are deployed. Scouts may use advanced optical cameras or a 180-degree mirror to discreetly peek around corners to locate suspects or determine their activity. The scout's job is to gather as much information as possible, including the suspects' location, prior to entry.

The Assaulter

The assaulters are members of the element that are responsible for making a forced entrance into a building and arresting suspects. They may use a battering ram to break down doors and be the first people of the element to enter the building.

The Element Leader

The element leader is normally the most experienced member on the assault team. He or she directs the tactical deployment of that element and is required to have a great understanding of all element member job duties and locations. The element leader must make quick and effective decisions under extreme pressure.

The Rear Guard

The rear guard is usually armed with a 12-gauge shotgun and is in charge of providing cover to the scout. He or she also helps gather information. The rear guard helps ensure that the scout does his or

Police officers monitor a hostage situation at a bank in Jackson, Mississippi, in April 1999. The lone gunman later released his hostages and was taken into custody.

her job unnoticed. If the scout is noticed, the guard helps him or her return to a safe position.

The Sniper

The sniper is a highly trained marksman who uses a target-grade rifle and scope to identify and observe suspects' movements. Whenever necessary, snipers must eliminate subjects who are a danger to innocent civilians or other officers. In order to avoid hitting victims or fellow officers, snipers must shoot accurately and possess excellent concentration skills. In addition, they must immediately know what to do in a variety of situations under extreme conditions. Snipers must sit for hours while focused. Because snipers may only get a single chance to hit their target, they practice for long hours under stressful conditions.

Snipers are also important for information gathering. In order to get detailed information about a crisis, snipers must sometimes get close to their targets using a hide. A hide is a carefully concealed location that makes it difficult for the suspect to locate the sniper,

Ballistic Helmet with Eye Protection

Nomex Hood (Balaclava)

MP-5 9mm. Submachine Gun

Radio with Tactical Communications System

Nomex Gloves

LBV: Load Bearing Vest (Not bulletproof)

Pistol

Gas Mask Pouch

This diagram shows some of the many weapons and other devices that SWAT team members make use of to keep the public safe and apprehend criminals in crisis situations.

but still provides a visual target. A sniper can describe a building's construction, the types of locks on its doors, and other very relevant information while secured in a hide. These details are relayed back to the command post and help the remaining team members understand the potential scenario. Accurate information gathering assists officers in many ways, especially when making decisions about what tools or weapons are needed for a successful entry. In most circumstances, accurate information gathering reduces the risk to bystanders.

The Spotter

A spotter helps the sniper identify targets and estimated distances, as well as other conditions that may affect the sniper's fire. The spotter also reports the result of any shots fired. In some circumstances the spotter may teargas subjects and is also responsible for radio communication and keeping a written record of SWAT activities. The spotter serves as the sniper's assistant and helps him or her perform with less distraction.

The SWAT Team Toolkit

Because SWAT teams must carry out specific missions, they also need specialized equipment to do their jobs well. From clothing and accessories to protective gear and weapons, a SWAT team's equipment is critical to the success of their mission.

Most SWAT teams use black fatigues, otherwise known as battle dress uniform (BDU). The BDUs are made from two-piece, tear-resistant heavy cotton that is treated with flame-retardant chemicals. SWAT team officers also wear a protective head covering, called a balaclava. Its design helps protect members from sparks and foreign objects that might otherwise injure them.

Body armor is used to protect officers from direct assaults. The load-bearing tactical vest provides protection against high-velocity ammunition and also offers a way to attach special equipment. Constructed out of a material called Kevlar, body armor is five times stronger than steel. An officer's ballistic helmet is also made from Kevlar, and can be equipped with a face shield for added protection. Some officers, usually the scout or the first officer on an element, also carry a shield. The KV-4 rectangular ballistic shield, for instance, is constructed with bullet-resistant glazing and has a view port so an officer can safely see through it without becoming exposed.

When a SWAT team needs to get into a building that has been barricaded or locked, the team uses two primary tools. The first, called a battering ram, is designed for use by one officer. It can break a door down quickly, allowing officers to enter a building while still maintaining an element of surprise. A hooligan tool, originally developed by fire departments to open doors, is used for prying open windows and loosening locks.

The SWAT team uses other tools to disable and confuse suspects. Defense Technology Corp Number 25 Distraction Devices

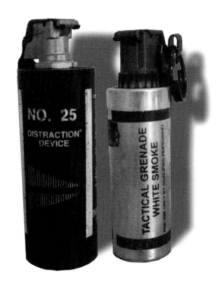

SWAT teams make use of flashbangs *(left)* and smoke grenades.

(flashbangs) are used to confuse or distract suspects by producing a very loud noise accompanied by a brilliant flash. A stingball is a flashbang that scatters rubber pellets when it's detonated. Stingballs are painful, but use nonlethal pellets that disperse rioting crowds. Tear gas, yet another method of exhausting suspects, will incapacitate them, forcing them to surrender. This saves officers from having to capture suspects by physical force. Because SWAT teams may use tear gas, officers always have gas masks readily available. Gas masks have large oval eyepieces, a changeable canister filter, and an exhalation valve that allows easier breathing and communication between officers.

As criminals become increasingly dangerous and prone to enter into shootouts with the police, law enforcement agencies must ensure that their weaponry keeps up with that of the criminals. The primary weapons used by SWAT teams in the United States are the .45 caliber Colt, the Heckler and Koch 9mm MP5 submachine gun (MP5 SMG), and the Benelli Super-90 12-gauge semiautomatic shotgun. The .45 caliber Colt has a long military history and is standard issue in many police forces. (Delta Force, the U.S. Army's elite counterterrorist special ops unit, uses a modified version.) The MP5 SMG is accurate, lightweight, and fast. It can fire 800 rounds per minute and weighs only five pounds unloaded. It is favored for close quarters and used by a number of law enforcement agencies and military special ops units.

Your Mission

4

Even though people sometimes associate SWAT teams with high-profile crimes like bank robberies and drug raids, like those seen in movies, they are called to the scene for a number of different situations. While high-profile situations may make exciting stories for Hollywood, the truth is that SWAT teams are often involved in many tedious events where nothing dramatic happens. This is sometimes true in hostage situations, for instance, where a SWAT team may spend hours at a scene before a peaceful surrender is negotiated. Because officers must be flexible in responding to various situations, they maintain a continual training schedule.

The most common occurences to which SWAT teams respond are listed below.

Distribution of SWAT Team Incidents

High-Risk Warrant — 49.7%

Barricade — 8.9%

Hostage Rescue — 1.9%

Dignitary Protection — 1.4%

Crowd Control/Civil Disorder — 1.3%

Training — 28.1%

Other — 9.0%

Barricaded Suspects

A barricaded suspect is someone who is armed, is dangerous to himself or to others, and has been involved in a criminal act or is considered a threat to citizens and police. His or her position is considered an advantaged one because it is concealed. Barricaded situations tend to be some of the most dangerous. Even though they are less likely to occur (8.9 percent of the incidents reported), the likelihood that someone will end up getting hurt or even killed is higher (18.6 percent of barricaded situations involve casualties), according to the Counter Narcotics and Terrorism Operational Medical Support Team (CONTOMS) program.

People barricade themselves in buildings for a number of different reasons, including trying to resist arrest. Other times their reasoning may be senseless. Because suspects are often running on adrenaline at the time of

A released hostage walks toward a SWAT unit at the Financial Exchange in Philadelphia where four gunmen took scores of people hostage after a failed robbery attempt in 1997.

Hostage Situations

A strange phenomenon sometimes occurs when captors hold hostages for long periods of time. Some hostages will eventually side with their captors and even attack police officers as they attempt to free them. Called the Stockholm Syndrome, it is defined as a psychological response to prolonged stress and fear. The hostages begin to believe in the suspects' cause, siding with them even though they are being held prisoner. The term "Stockholm Syndrome" comes from an attempted bank robbery in 1973 in Stockholm, Sweden. After being held for more than six days in a bank vault, four hostages developed strong emotional bonds with their captors and actually attempted to protect them from arrest.

the incident and are highly agitated, SWAT teams and negotiators must be patient and coax them into surrendering themselves. This avoids additional danger to the officers' lives and often saves the lives of the suspects.

In certain incidents, a SWAT team is called when a suspect is holding hostages under a threat of violence. Sometimes it may involve an estranged person the suspect knows or, in other cases, a stranger, like during a bank robbery. In situations such as this, it could be people who just happened to be in the building when the police cornered the suspect. In other cases, hostages are taken specifically with the intent of gaining something in return, such as ransom. Regardless of the reason, SWAT teams have to quickly identify the situation and decide the most appropriate method for handling it.

In most instances, a negotiator is used to communicate with suspects. Because suspects are excited when they initially find themselves in a hostage situation, it may take time before they realize their own foolishness. Some opt to leave with dignity and surrender. Hostage negotiators can help suspects come to terms with what they have done. Very often the key to a peaceful surrender is careful administration and diligence by a SWAT negotiator.

As a last resort, a SWAT team may need to infiltrate a location to subdue the suspects. This is extremely dangerous for everyone involved, and is an option only when hostages' lives are at risk.

High-Risk Warrant Service

SWAT teams spend the majority of their time serving warrants, risking injury or even death in many cases. Because of the extreme penalties of arrest and conviction, some criminals take risks trying to escape or fighting the police while being served with a warrant. This is obviously never a good idea. When zeroing in on a suspect who has decided to take flight, SWAT teams are necessary to overwhelm the criminal's firepower in order to make the arrest safely.

Special Incidence Units

T here are a number of other people and special teams who assist the SWAT team. Some are police officers who offer support, while others are particular units who work with the SWAT team if a specific problem is encountered. For example, if a SWAT team is dealing with a potentially explosive device, the bomb squad will assist them with the process of defusing it.

The Crisis Negotiation Team

In certain circumstances, a crisis negotiation team (CNT) may be used to handle a barricaded suspect. The CNT is comprised of specialized SWAT officers and other personnel who are trained in negotiation

Vermont police tried for sixteen hours to negotiate with a man who fired seventy rounds of ammunition inside his home. The man, who was upset after a dispute with his girlfriend, eventually killed himself.

skills. A CNT also has five members: a team supervisor, primary and secondary negotiators, a psychologist, and an investigator. The CNT will establish communication with the suspect in order to arrange for the safe release of hostages.

K-9 Unit

Animals also risk their lives to protect innocent people. Dogs are an invaluable asset to police and SWAT teams in special circumstances. Just like people, it takes a special type of dog to perform in a K-9 unit. Typically, German shepherds, Belgian Malinois, or Dutch shepherds are used by police since they have the appropriate temperament to handle patrol work and the stress that comes with it.

Dogs are used to help locate suspects or find drugs. For instance, police dogs are commonly trained to find toys that have drugs hidden inside them. By using scent, dogs learn to locate the toy by smell, just as many pet dogs would when searching for their favorite ball. When the dogs are in the field, they use their noses to find their "toy"—the drugs hidden in a suspect's car, on his or her body, or in a building.

Paramedic Unit

Paramedics provide close support to SWAT teams. Depending on where they work, they may have to pass the federal CONTOMS program sponsored by the Department of Defense. Paramedics train with SWAT members to ensure they understand their role and how to function within the team. Because the paramedics' role on the team is that of medical support, they are

unarmed and positioned by the SWAT team commander as necessary.

Paramedics can offer immediate assistance to victims or any members of the SWAT team who are
harmed in an event. Paramedics monitor each member
of the team closely. They also track and report information so that they can offer better support in the future. If
an officer is wounded, a paramedic will have his or her
information readily available and can start treating that
officer immediately. Otherwise, if assisting an officer is
potentially dangerous, paramedics must wait until the
area is secured completely.

Bomb Squad

Bomb squads are used when incidents involve sus-
pected explosive devices. Like any other specialized
team, the members must receive fresh training on a
regular basis. To become an accredited bomb squad
member, each person on the team must complete
special training at the FBI's Hazardous Devices
School. Bomb squad members may also help citizens
and business owners through special training that

deals with bomb threats or identifying explosives and explosive devices.

Hazmat Team

A hazmat, or hazardous materials, team assists when a crisis involves dangerous substances. This could be a chemical leak or explosion, dangerous

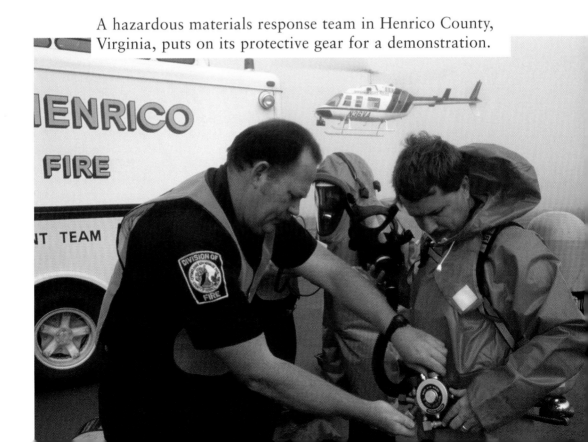

A hazardous materials response team in Henrico County, Virginia, puts on its protective gear for a demonstration.

and flammable liquids or gases, or the release of fuel and other illegal hazardous materials or biological agents. Like other groups, the hazmat team has to complete and pass regular training exercises (usually four times a year) and receive special certifications annually. These teams also train local firefighters and support agencies that might be the first rescuers on the scene of an emergency.

Victim Assistance Advocates

Sometimes it seems that once a crisis is off the front page of the newspaper, it's over. Unfortunately, that's hardly ever the case. After a SWAT team has averted a dangerous situation, investigations begin, reports are written, and many people who were involved need additional help. Released hostages and their families often need assistance dealing with the effects of a crisis after it's over, even if no one is hurt. Victim assistance advocates often arrive on the scene of a crisis and help by counseling those involved and offering whatever support they can. These problem solvers help in any way possible, from finding shelter to providing clothing and food. Victim assistance advocates may hold a series of follow-up meetings with the victims to see how they are coping, or help in simple ways such as offering someone a ride home.

Police officers also need time to readjust after a particularly stressful episode. They, and those who support them, often deal with people in the worst situations, when normally rational people are behaving poorly. Because of this, it is very important for officers to find a way to cope with job stress. In order to remain healthy, police departments sometimes offer peer support groups, where officers discuss their concerns with fellow officers.

On the Job

SWAT team members who are on-call are required to be available at a moment's notice. Twenty-four hours a day, no matter where they are, officers must arrive at a situation quickly. Some are given an off-duty cruiser or have outfitted their own vehicles so they can approach a scene quickly. When SWAT team members are on-call, they are usually restricted to traveling within a certain distance of their designated area.

Responding to a Call

When the SWAT team responds to a call, they usually gather to discuss the plan of action and receive directions from their element leader. One of the first things the team has to do is gather as much relevant information as possible. Often the element leader will personally review an incident. This gives him or her an opportunity to assess what actions may be necessary. Because officers aren't usually onsite when the crisis begins, the team speaks with other personnel who arrived there first and who can provide information in greater detail. As the team collects and organizes that data, they assess the information with assistance from other command post personnel and develop a tactical plan.

A command post is usually set up within close proximity to where a crisis is occurring. Some SWAT teams actually have their own mobile command posts. This may be a large van or mobile home, fitted with all of the communication devices and equipment that the SWAT team and supporting personnel may require. It is important to adequately secure the command post since local media may, in some cases, broadcast the SWAT team's intentions. If the suspect is watching television or listening to a radio from inside a location, he or she may hear information about a SWAT team's movements before they do anything. This can obviously put officers at risk and ruin the effectiveness of any planned actions or negotiations.

Because police officers are most likely the first to arrive on the scene, it is up to those officers to set up perimeters and prepare for the arrival of the

The Albuquerque SWAT team gets ready to enter a Marriott hotel after three people, a woman and her two children, were found shot to death on the fourteenth floor of the building in January 2001.

remaining team. To successfully protect the sur-
rounding area, maintain control over the situation,
and allow the SWAT team and others involved in
the crisis to work efficiently, police personnel do a
number of different things.

Safety is the primary concern in any of these
situations. Therefore, the police spend time setting
up perimeters and security, even if the outcome
is expected to be harmless. For example, if the
SWAT team is serving a warrant or is in a barricade
situation, they don't want people milling around and
walking in and out of the secured area. The police
must control onlookers and media coverage,
and ensure the safety of bystanders who might not
realize they are in danger.

Assault and Rescue

As a last resort, a SWAT team may be required to use
force to enter a building and apprehend a suspect
hiding inside. Obviously, this is done only if there
are no options left, especially if the suspect has
placed hostages at risk or has injured them. In many
cases, a SWAT team simply overwhelms a suspect

SWAT team officers from Florida's Monroe County Sheriff's
Department search a hallway during a training exercise.

until he or she realizes that resistance is useless. Other times, a SWAT team may be forced to deal with the suspect physically, which is never in the suspect's best interests.

Depending upon the situation, a SWAT team may overwhelm a suspect using either dynamic entry or stealth (secret) entry. A dynamic entry is used if there is an immediate threat to a hostage, or if other obstacles prevent a stealth entry. In a dynamic entry, the SWAT team forces a sudden entrance into a location using battering rams or explosives to open door locks or windows. At the same time, other members of the SWAT team use diversions to distract and confuse the suspect from what the SWAT team is doing.

A stealth entry, on the other hand, is used to surround and contain a suspect without him or her knowing it. The use of stealth entry requires the team to move very carefully and quietly, and is used if the team doesn't know where exactly a suspect is located. If hostages aren't in immediate danger, or if the building is very large, a stealth entry is effective.

Police SWAT Teams: Life on High Alert

SWAT teams have an engagement sequence that is practiced over and over until it becomes automatic in a crisis situation. The engagement sequence generally comprises eight steps:

1. Locate the target.

2. Get into a stable position.

3. Estimate the range to the target.

4. Optically confirm the target.

5. Estimate the wind.

6. Aim and fire.

7. Follow through and reload.

8. Engage other targets as needed.

Safety is always a SWAT team's primary concern. While officers train endlessly, sometimes no amount of training can fully prepare them for an actual situation. SWAT teams work like any other team does: They depend upon their most experienced leaders and help other members in times of trouble. Experience, more than any other skill, lends itself to an effective SWAT force.

Mission Complete!

7

$\mathcal{S}$WAT team members perform a job that is unlike any other. For most people, a workday that ends at 5:00 PM leaves them free to do whatever they please on their own time. SWAT members who are on-call constantly sacrifice their personal time. Even after a day on the job, they may be called back to help in an emergency. Officers routinely go above and beyond the normal confines of a "job" to ensure that the public remains safe.

Even after perfecting a skill, SWAT team members continue training for long hours. If they don't, they may become sloppy in their work, lazy, or perhaps even injured. In order to protect themselves, their colleagues, and the public, SWAT team members constantly practice in order to remain fully trained, efficient, and sharper than any potential criminal.

Brenda Konfrst of the Omaha SWAT team holds her
one-year-old son, Jacob, after he watched her in a SWAT
demonstration in May 2001.

To Protect Another Day

SWAT team members, like police officers, are very valuable individuals who sacrifice a great deal to ensure the safety of others. These people are sometimes overlooked by society. They must be willing to consistently train, learn, and think about their job. Being part of a SWAT team, or even a member of a police squad, requires cooperation and support from family and friends.

Like other jobs that require individuals to go beyond the call of duty, these positions can be very rewarding for the individuals holding them. Even if public servants are sometimes overlooked, they are diligent heroes to the thousands of people they protect on a daily basis.

Glossary

balaclava A protective head covering worn alone or under a helmet.

ballistic helmet Made from Kevlar, a helmet that protects an officer's head and that can be equipped with a face shield for extra protection.

ballistic shield A protective shield constructed with a bullet-resistant glazing and a view port so that an officer can see from behind it.

battering ram A large, wooden beam used to gain entry through locked doors or barriers. It can be operated by a single officer and usually weighs around thirty pounds.

battle dress uniform (BDU) Two-piece, tear-resistant clothing made from heavy cotton treated with a special flame retardant.

call-up The act of being on alert twenty-four hours a day. An officer who is on call-up has to be on the scene quickly and must be available at all hours.

dynamic (sudden) entry A SWAT team response when there is immediate danger to a hostage, or if other obstacles prevent a stealth entry.

element A SWAT team's basic five-person unit.

engagement sequence A practiced routine by which officers automatically perform their duties.

flashbang A device used to confuse or distract suspects. It emits a very loud noise accompanied by a brilliant flash.

gas mask A rubber mask used to protect against toxic gases. It has a changeable filter that helps remove foreign substances from the air, and an exhalation valve that allows officers to breathe and communicate.

hooligan tool First developed by fire departments, a tool that lets officers open entrances into buildings by prying out windows or loosening locks.

Kevlar A fibrous material, five times stronger than steel, that is used in body armor.

load-bearing tactical vest A body armor vest that protects against high-velocity ammunition.

POST The Police Officer Standard Test. Police cadets

are required to pass the POST prior to acceptance into a police department.

stealth entry Methods used when a SWAT team needs to surround and contain a suspect without him or her becoming aware that he or she is surrounded.

stingball A type of flashbang that scatters nonlethal rubber pellets when discharged.

Stockholm Syndrome A psychological response to prolonged stress and fear that causes hostages to side with their captors.

surveillance Keeping close watch over someone or something.

tear gas A gas that will incapacitate a suspect to the point where he or she surrenders.

For More Information

Counter Narcotics & Terrorism Operational Medical
    Support (CONTOMS)
Casualty Care Research Center
4301 Jones Bridge Road
Bethesda, MD 20814-4799
(301) 295-6263
Web site: http://www.usuhs.mil/ccr/ccrc_main_page.htm

National Tactical Officers Association
P.O. Box 797
Doylestown, PA 18901
(800) 279-9127
Web site: http://www.ntoa.org/

Web Sites

Due to the changing nature of Internet links, the Rosen Publishing Group, Inc., has developed an online list of Web sites related to the subject of this book. This site is updated regularly. Please use this link to access the list:

http://www.rosenlinks.com/eca/post/

For Further Reading

Boraas, Tracy. *Police Detective* (Career Explorations). Mankato, MN: Capstone Press, 2001.

Burgan, Michael. *U.S. Navy Special Forces: Special Boat Units* (Warfare and Weapons). Mankato, MN: Capstone Press, 2000.

Halberstadt, Hans. *Swat Team: Police Special Weapons and Tactics* (Power Series). Osceola, WI: Motorbooks International, 1994.

Katz, Samuel M. *LAPD: Patrol, SWAT, Air Support, K-9, Crash and Homicide* (Power Series). Osceola, WI: Motorbooks International, 1997.

Needles, Collen, Kit Carlson, and Kim Levin. *Working Dogs: Tales from Animal Planet's K-9 to 5 World.* Hamilton, MT: Discovery Books, 2000.

Snow, Robert L. *Swat Teams: Explosive Face-Offs with America's Deadliest Criminals.* Cambridge, MA: Perseus Publishing, 2000.

Bibliography

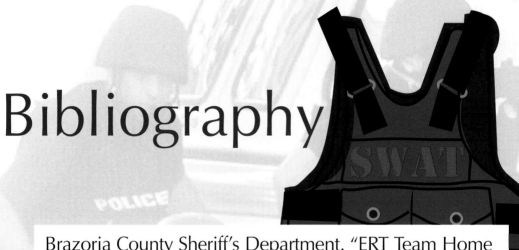

Brazoria County Sheriff's Department. "ERT Team Home Page." 2002. Retrieved February 14, 2002 (http://www.brazoria-county.com/sheriff/ERT_pages/).

Casey, James C. "Directory of Police SWAT Teams." 2001. Retrieved October 1, 2001 (http://www.policeguide.com/swat.htm).

City of Columbia Police Department. "Columbia, Missouri Police STAR Team." 2002. Retrieved February 14, 2002 (http://www.ci.columbia.mo.us/ dept/police/ starhome.htm).

Douglas County Sheriff's Office. "S.W.A.T." 2001. Retrieved October 1, 2001 (http://www.douglas.co.us/sheriff/Divisions/Patrol/ SWAT.htm).

El Paso County. "Sheriff's Office SWAT, El Paso County, CO." 2001. Retrieved October 1, 2001 (http://www.co.el-paso.co.us/sheriff/swat.htm).

Federal Interagency Council on Statistical Policy. "FedStats: Crime Statistics." 2001. Retrieved October 1, 2001 (http://www.fedstats.gov/ programs/crime.html).

Katz, Samuel M. "Felon Busters." 1997. Retrieved February 14, 2002 (http:// popularmechanics.com/ science/law_enforcement/1997/5/lapd_swat/ print.phtml).

Massachusetts Department of State Police. "Special Emergency Response Team." 2002. Retrieved February 14, 2002 (http://www.state.ma.us/ msp/unitpage/sert.htm).

National Tactical Officers Association. Retrieved February 14, 2002 (http://www.ntoa.org).

SitesNow! Development Team One. "North American Police Work Dog Association." 1998. Retrieved October 1, 2001 (http://www.napwda.com).

SpecWarNet. "TacLink—Training & Resources." 2000. Retrieved October 1, 2001 (http://www.specwarnet.com/taclink/Schools).

TacLink. "TacLink—MedStar Tactical Medics." 2002. Retrieved February 14, 2002 (http://www.-specwarnet.com/taclink/Medics/medstar.htm).

Index

About the Author

Christopher D. Goranson, a resident of Denver, Colorado, spends most of his leisure time enjoying the great outdoors with his fiancée, Lindsay.

Photo Credits

Cover, pp. 29, 48 © Monroe County Sheriff's Department, Florida; p. 8 © Bob Flora/UPI/Bettmann/Corbis; p. 9 © Bettmann/Corbis; pp. 12, 17, 19, 22, 24, 26, 29, 33, 38, 46, 52 © AP/Photo Wide World; p. 41 © Tim Wright/Corbis. Rosen Publishing Group would like to acknowledge the help of the Monroe County Sheriff's Department for their assistance with some of the images in this book.

Design and Layout

Les Kanturek